A gift for:
From:

D0966320

Hang In 'Til the

Miracle Happens

Ruth Fishel

ILLUSTRATED BY BONNY VAN DE KAMP

MJF BOOKS | NEW YORK

Published by MJF Books
Fine Communications
322 Eighth Avenue
New York, NY 10001

Hang In 'Til the Miracle Happens
LC Control Number: 2011932148
ISBN–13: 978–1–60671–058–6
ISBN–10: 1–60671–058–3

This edition is published by MJF Books in arrangement with Spirithaven.

Designed by Lisa Chovnick

Printed in Singapore

TWP 10 9 8 7 6 5 4 3 2 1

Dear Reader:

This book, HANG IN 'TIL THE MIRACLE HAPPENS, was first published in 1992, one of four small books in a series entitled Meditative Moments. It was extremely well received and sold over 40,000 copies within a very short period of time.

There are a few reasons that I am honored and delighted that Fine Creative Media, Inc., has seen the value of the book and has decided to republish it.

Over the years I have received numerous calls and letters from readers thanking me for HANG IN 'TIL THE MIRACLE HAPPENS and telling me how much it has helped them manage many difficult circumstances in their lives. And, after all these years, I still receive calls and e-mails from people asking where the book can be purchased.

The other reason, certainly no less important than the first, is that this book is very special to my heart. When I originally submitted the book to the publisher, I had not yet written the dedication. Around 7:00 p.m. on October 12, 1992, I received the shocking news that Bob Fishel, my 29-year-old son, had ended his life. I remember one of my very first thoughts was that I wished so much I had sent Bob a copy of the manuscript. It might have helped! But I had no idea he was so troubled or would make such a final, tragic, irreversible decision. The book was going to press just hours before I left the house for his funeral. I can still see myself standing at my dining room table when the inspiration came for the dedication. I have no idea how I had the presence of mind to call, but I dialed the publisher and whispered the two-sentence dedication that had come to me.

So now, I present to you HANG IN 'TIL THE MIRACLE HAPPENS again. May it be a guide, an inspiration, and a light for you when you are going through a rough time, when you feel down or depressed, or when you simply need some hope.

With Love and Peace,

Ruth Fishel

Ellenton, Florida
May 2011

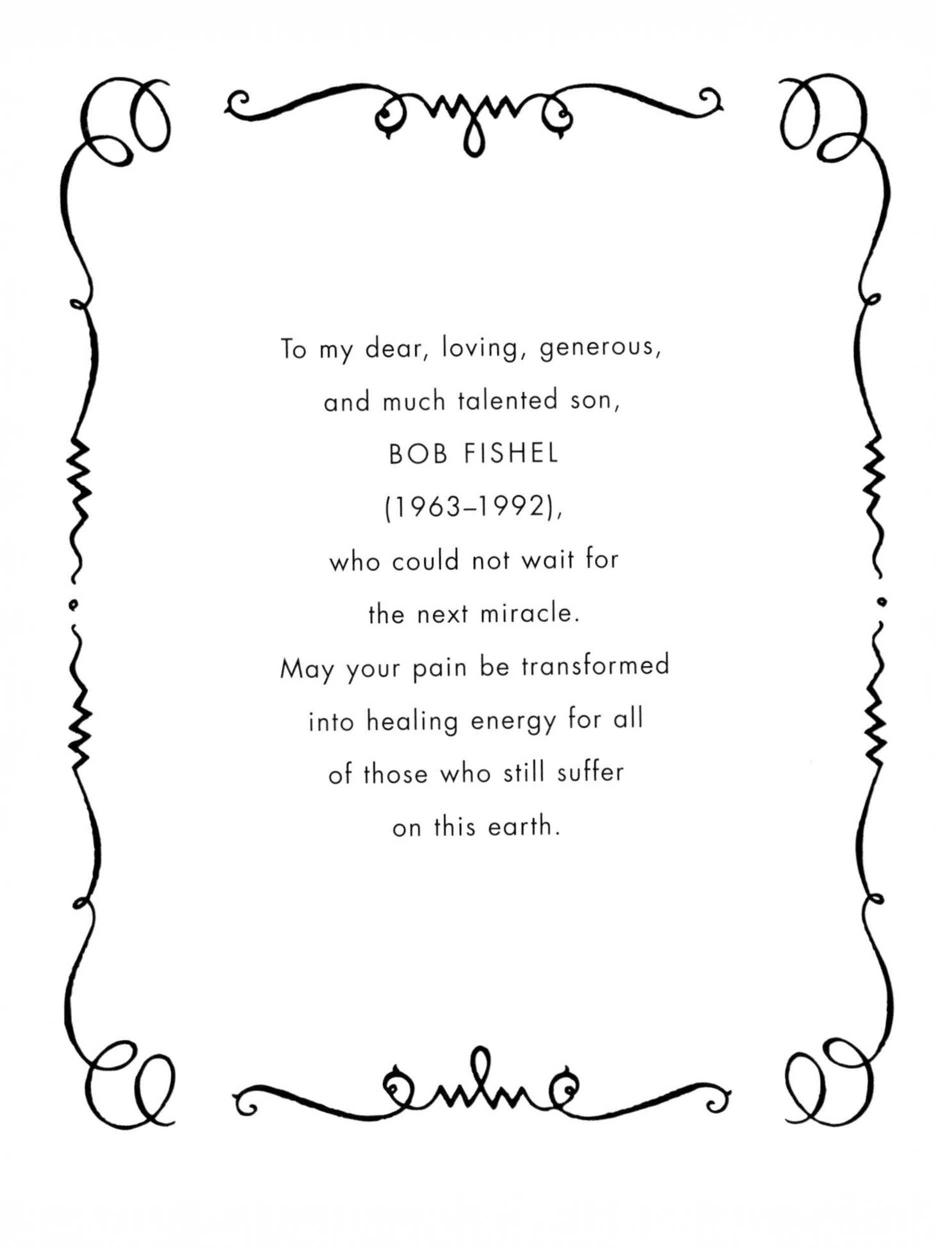

To my dear, loving, generous,
and much talented son,
BOB FISHEL
(1963–1992),
who could not wait for
the next miracle.
May your pain be transformed
into healing energy for all
of those who still suffer
on this earth.

Hang In 'Til the

Miracle Happens

here i am.

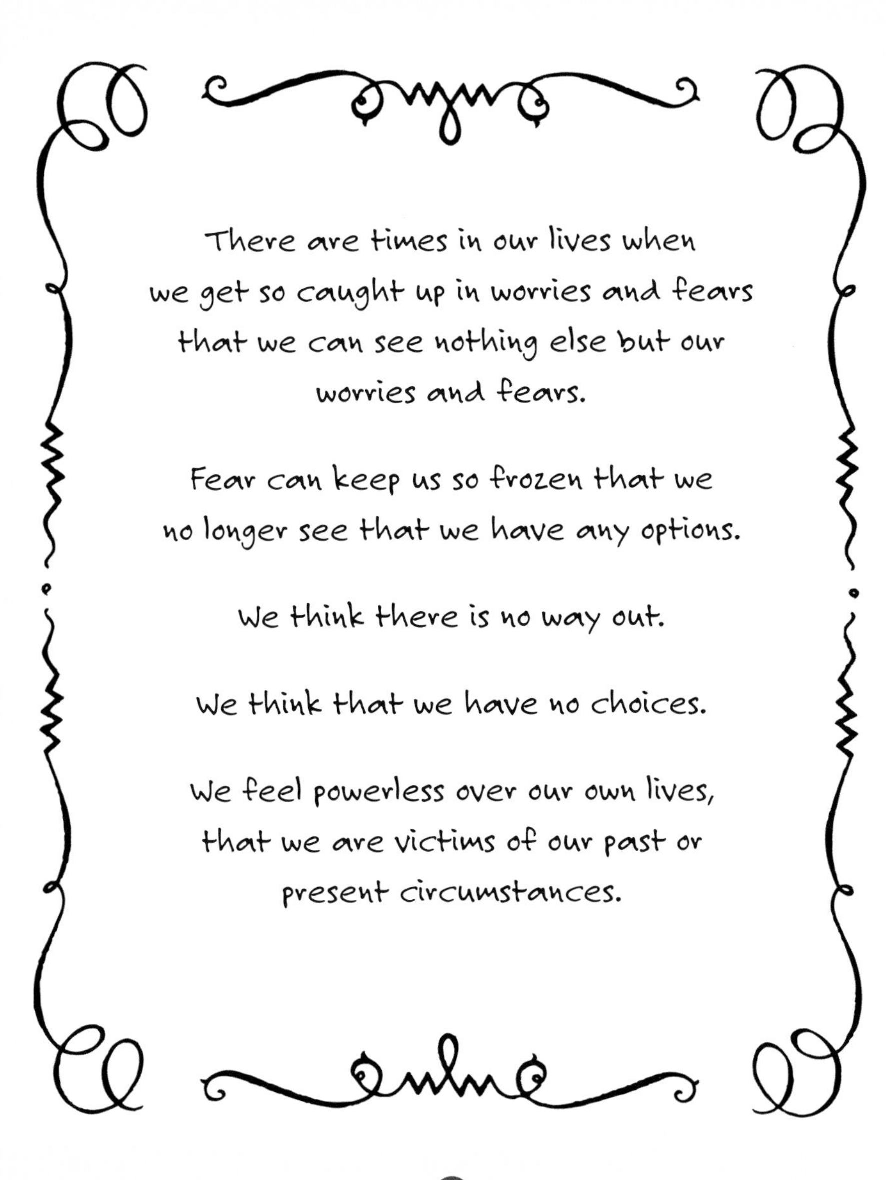

There are times in our lives when
we get so caught up in worries and fears
that we can see nothing else but our
worries and fears.

Fear can keep us so frozen that we
no longer see that we have any options.

We think there is no way out.

We think that we have no choices.

We feel powerless over our own lives,
that we are victims of our past or
present circumstances.

There are times when we feel we
don't seem to fit anywhere . . . not with
our family or friends or ourselves . . .
not even with God.

There are even times when

we feel like giving up.

Yet other times our
hearts can soar!

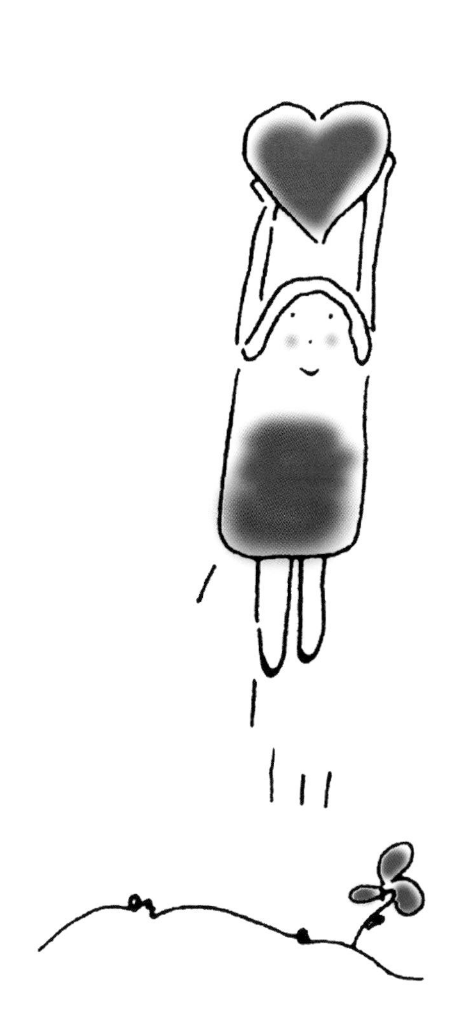

you and me...

These are the times when we
think we hold the power of the world
in the palm of our hand.

We want to sing and dance and
shout with the joy of life.

We feel invincible, indestructible,
powerful . . . as if we can
do no wrong!

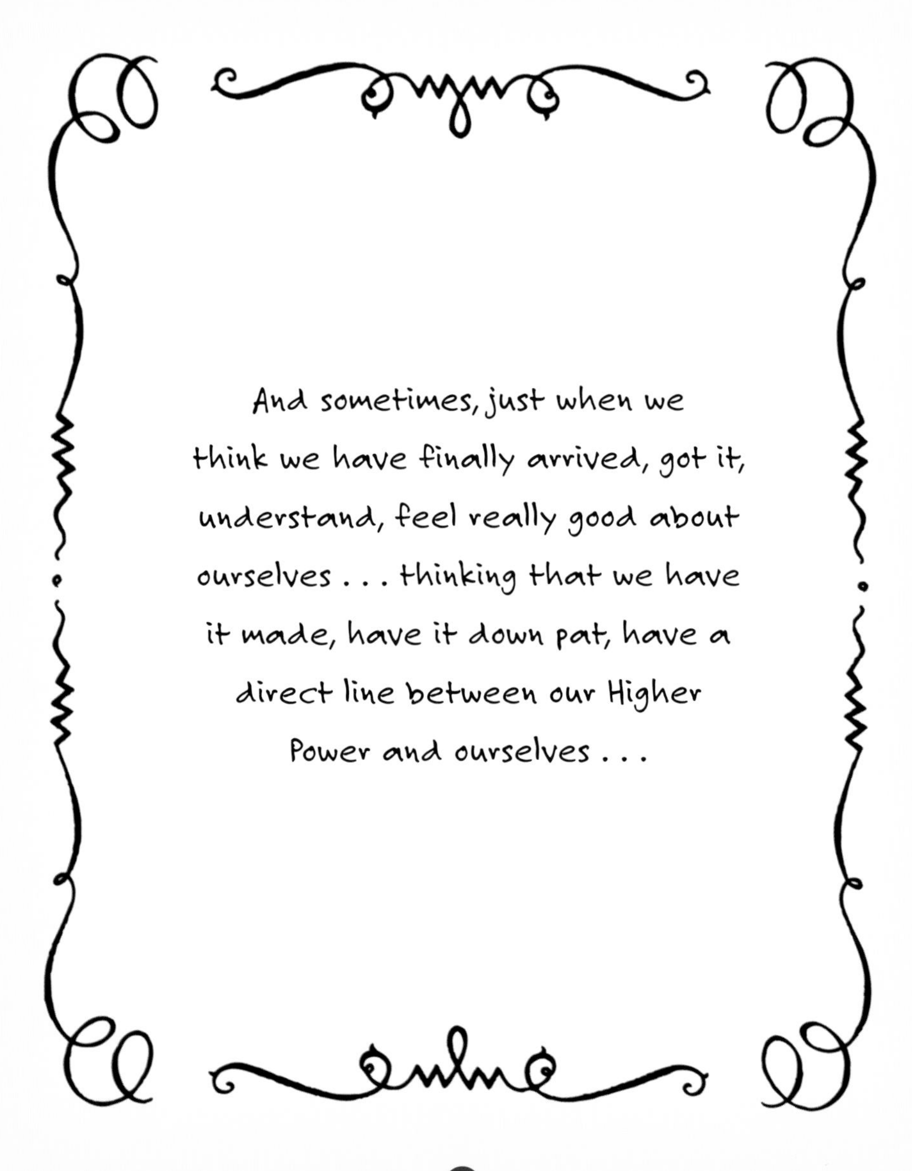

And sometimes, just when we
think we have finally arrived, got it,
understand, feel really good about
ourselves . . . thinking that we have
it made, have it down pat, have a
direct line between our Higher
Power and ourselves . . .

CRASH!!!

All the old feelings come back . . .

TENFOLD!

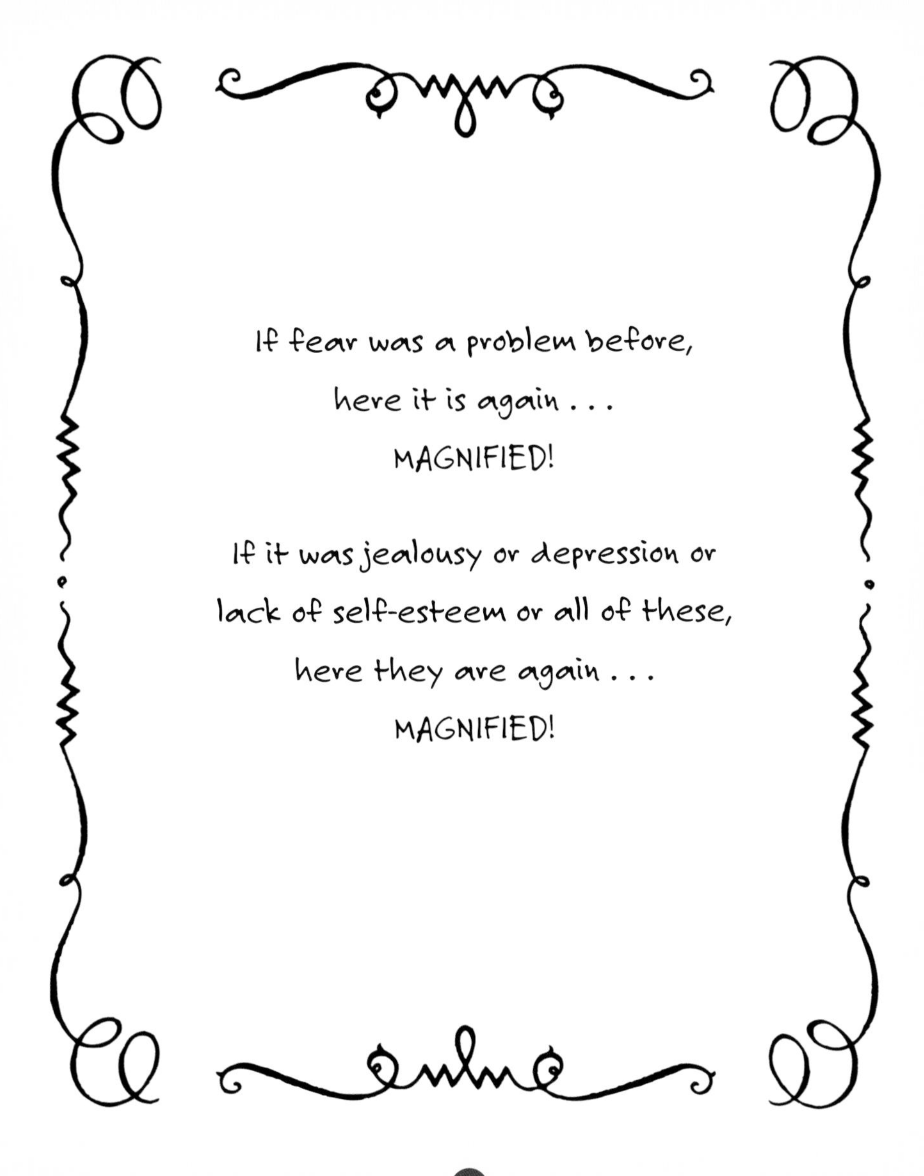

If fear was a problem before,

here it is again . . .

MAGNIFIED!

If it was jealousy or depression or

lack of self-esteem or all of these,

here they are again . . .

MAGNIFIED!

Maybe you have found new
bothersome feelings that you
didn't know existed!

And you wonder . . .

What did I do wrong?

Consider this another
opportunity to examine the patterns
that ended in trouble before
and keep you stuck now.

In this new light you have an opportunity to see these patterns and to become willing to let them go.

Perhaps new situations have occurred
in your life and nothing exists in your
conscious awareness that you can
tie in to these feelings.

time to move on!

Life certainly has a way of keeping us on our toes, keeping us from becoming complacent, and pushing us to move on and grow.

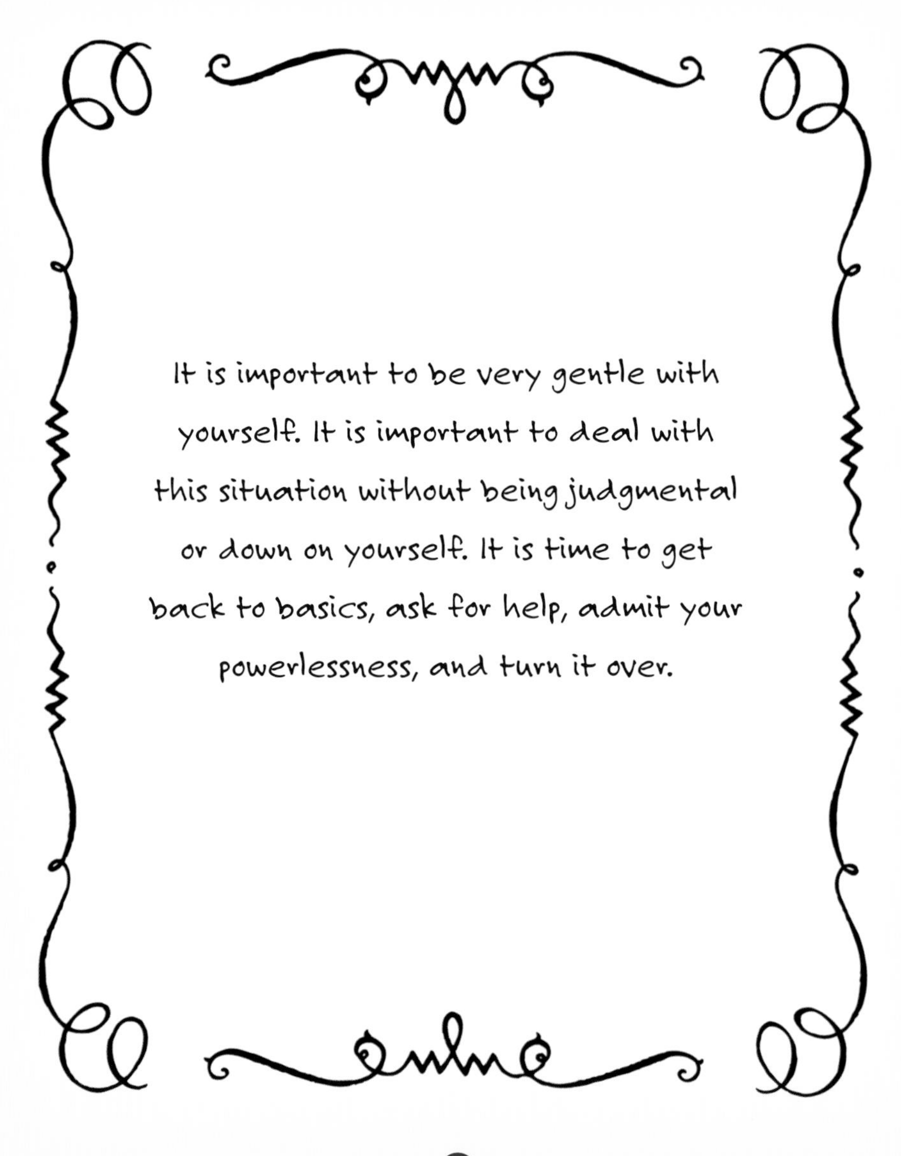

It is important to be very gentle with yourself. It is important to deal with this situation without being judgmental or down on yourself. It is time to get back to basics, ask for help, admit your powerlessness, and turn it over.

Why do we feel one way on one day
and totally different on another?

Why do our moods shift so quickly?

Why are we so affected by our circumstances that we feel as if we have fallen from the top of the world to the bottom? From light to darkness? From joy to despair?

Why do we sometimes feel as
if we can handle all things and
other times the most simple
thing feels impossible?

Maybe we'll never really
know all of the WHYS?

Maybe it is genetic
or environmental
or societal
or . . .
or . . .
or . . . .

Does it really matter?

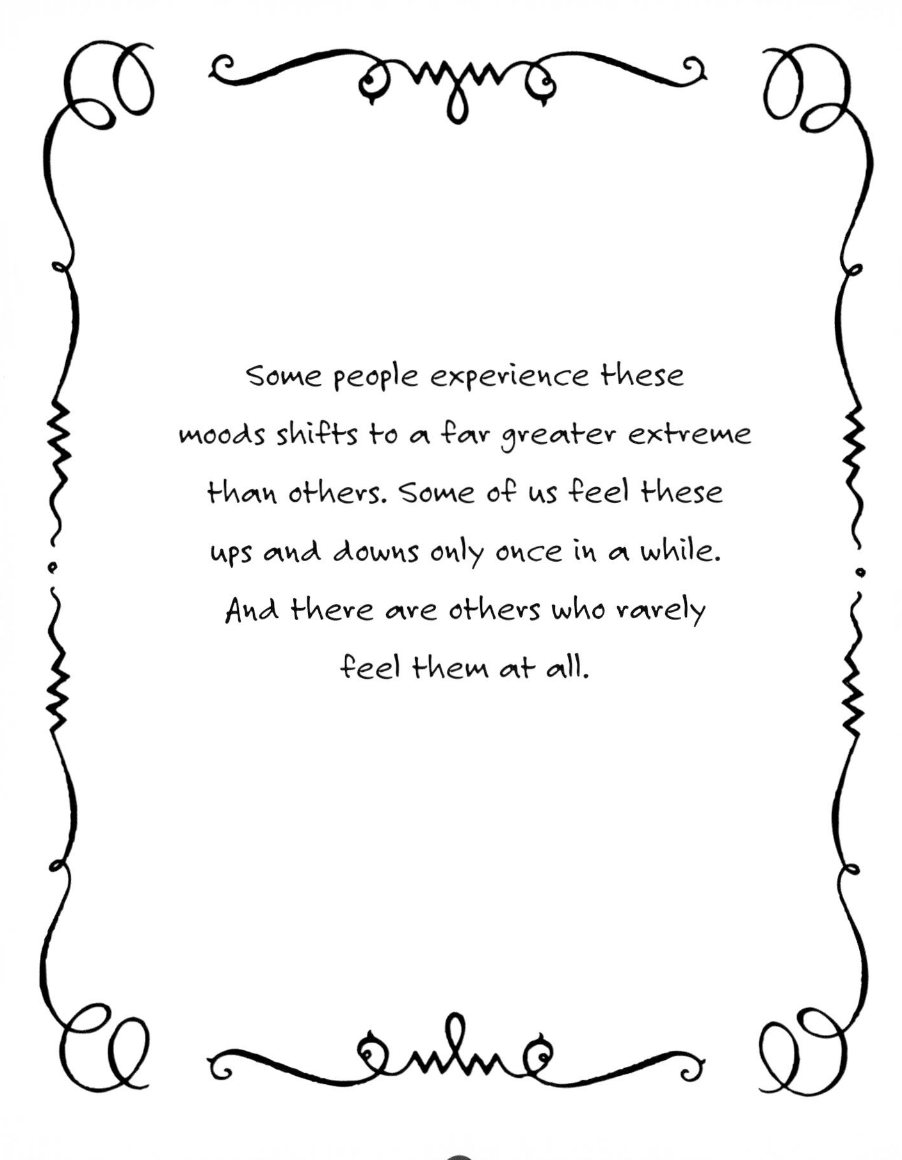

Some people experience these moods shifts to a far greater extreme than others. Some of us feel these ups and downs only once in a while. And there are others who rarely feel them at all.

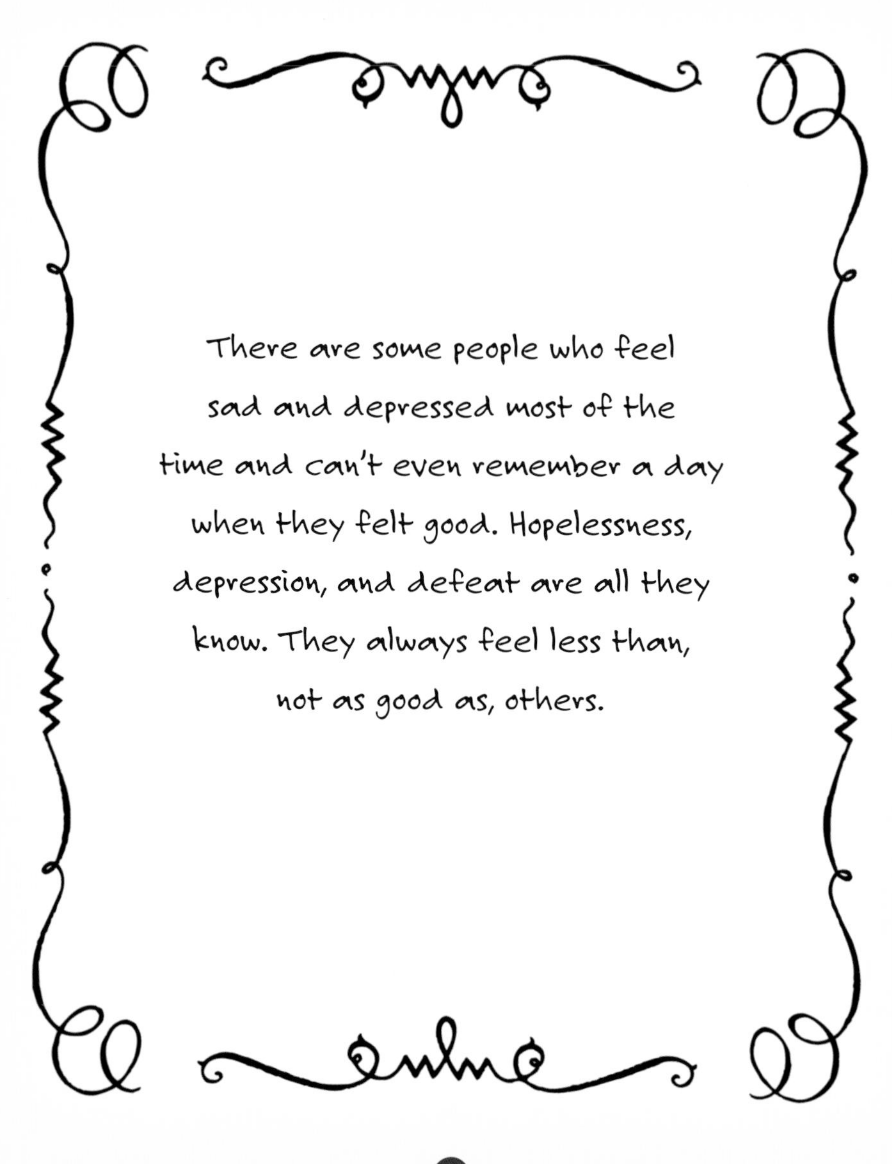

There are some people who feel
sad and depressed most of the
time and can't even remember a day
when they felt good. Hopelessness,
depression, and defeat are all they
know. They always feel less than,
not as good as, others.

Whatever the case might be for you, let this little book be like a friend in your pocket, a friend that is always with you.

Whenever you feel low or sad, fearful or defeated, or just plain powerless, know that you can pause and turn to this book to become centered and reconnect with your inner spirit. It will bring you back to a place where you can connect with a Power that is always with you, a Power that is greater than yourself.

Sometimes just stopping
what you are doing for a minute
can lift your spirits.

What does it mean to have
our spirits lifted?

Imagine that there is a spark of light within you. Imagine that spark is barely visible; that through pain and disappointment, this spark has been covered up, and that it shines only dimly now.

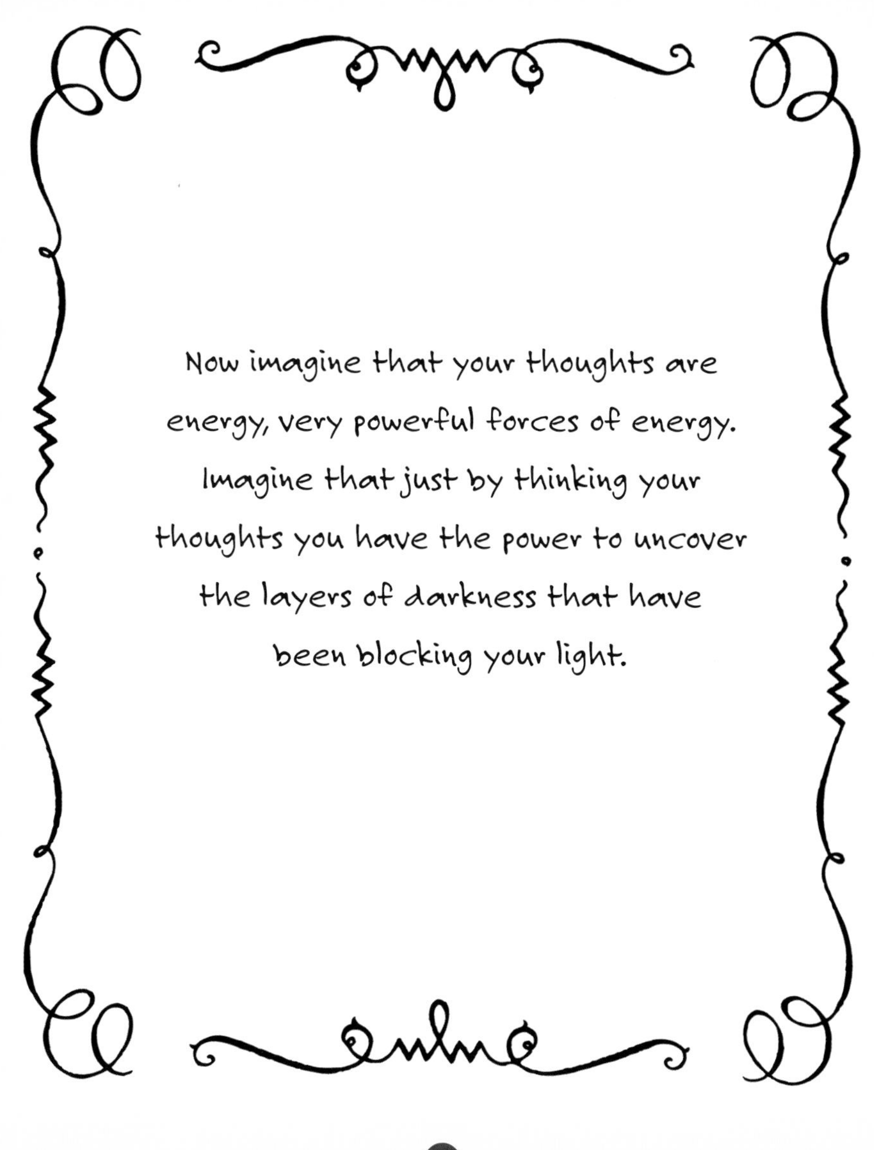

Now imagine that your thoughts are
energy, very powerful forces of energy.
Imagine that just by thinking your
thoughts you have the power to uncover
the layers of darkness that have
been blocking your light.

Now imagine this light shining through. Imagine it shining through and warming you, giving you energy.

Let yourself feel the power from the light of your inner spirit.

Know that we are all connected by that same spark of life. Let's just take a moment to think about that.

yes!

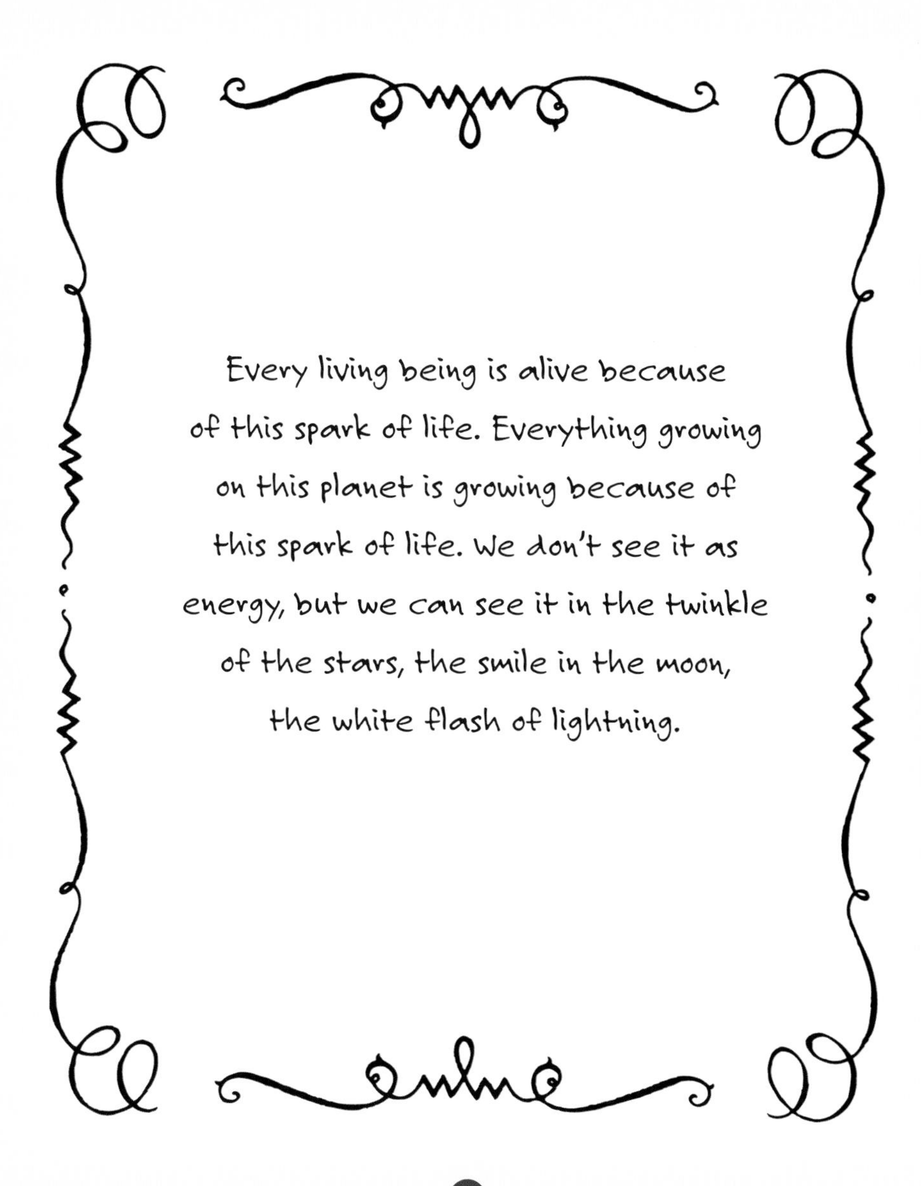

Every living being is alive because of this spark of life. Everything growing on this planet is growing because of this spark of life. We don't see it as energy, but we can see it in the twinkle of the stars, the smile in the moon, the white flash of lightning.

We can't actually smell it but it shows
up in the wonderful aroma of the flowers
and grass and ocean breezes.

We can even feel it in the smile of
a stranger, the magic of a butterfly
landing on a flower just inches away,
the power of a sunrise, the
glow of a sunset.

We can't actually hear it, but
it is there when we hear the crash
of thunder, the flickering of flames
in a bonfire, waves smashing
against the rocks;

when we hear the power of a
hurricane race by, the force of strong
winds shaking acorns from the branches,
the gentle song of soft breezes rustling
dry leaves in autumn.

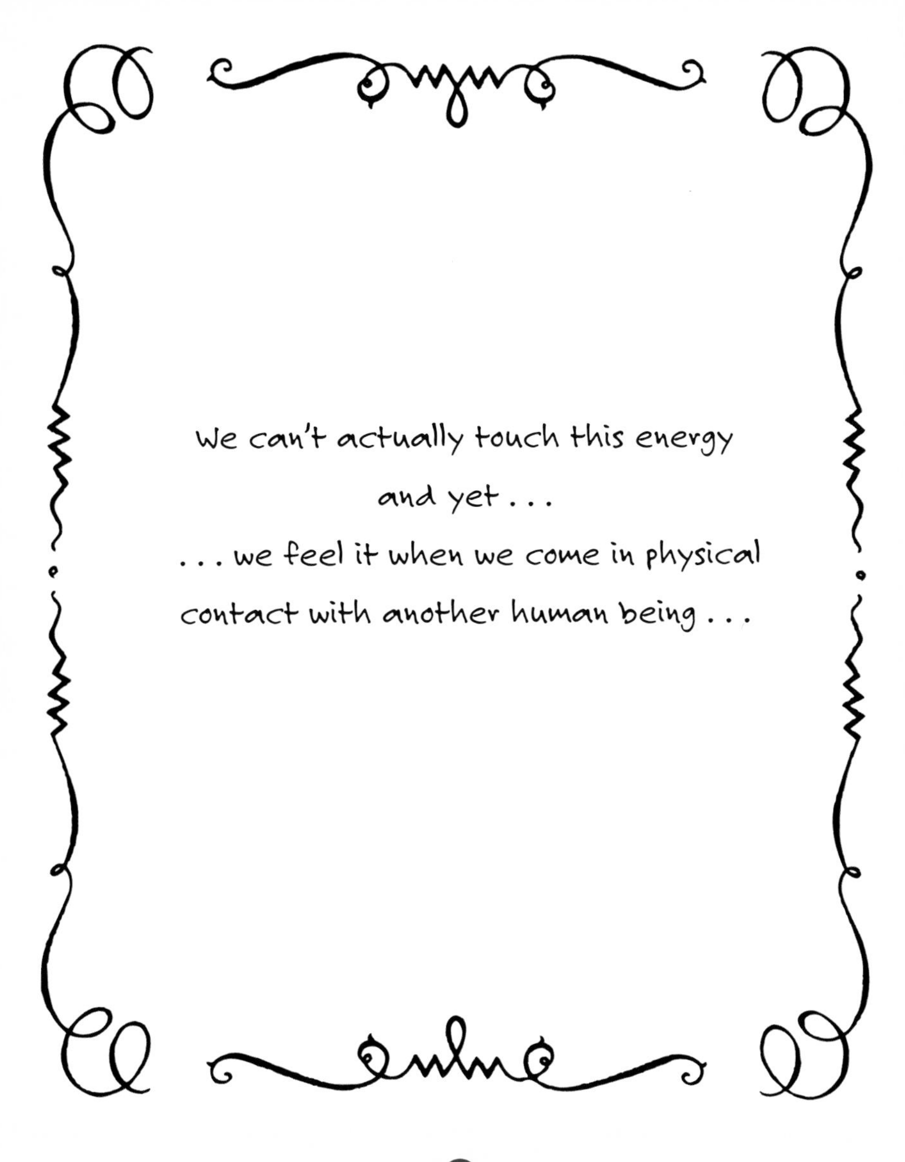

we can't actually touch this energy

and yet . . .

. . . we feel it when we come in physical

contact with another human being . . .

When we gently hold a baby . . .

Or let a caterpillar crawl
in the palm of our hand,

when we feel the moist earth, when we
plant seeds with our bare hands.

joy!

Contact.

Connection.

Connectedness.

Picture yourself lying next to a purring kitten. Feel the vibration of her sounds against the contact places where she connects with your body.

it's about change!

Imagine spring
changing into summer
changing into autumn
changing into winter
changing into spring
again.

Imagine warm
changing into hot
changing into cool
changing into cold
changing into warm
again.

yum!

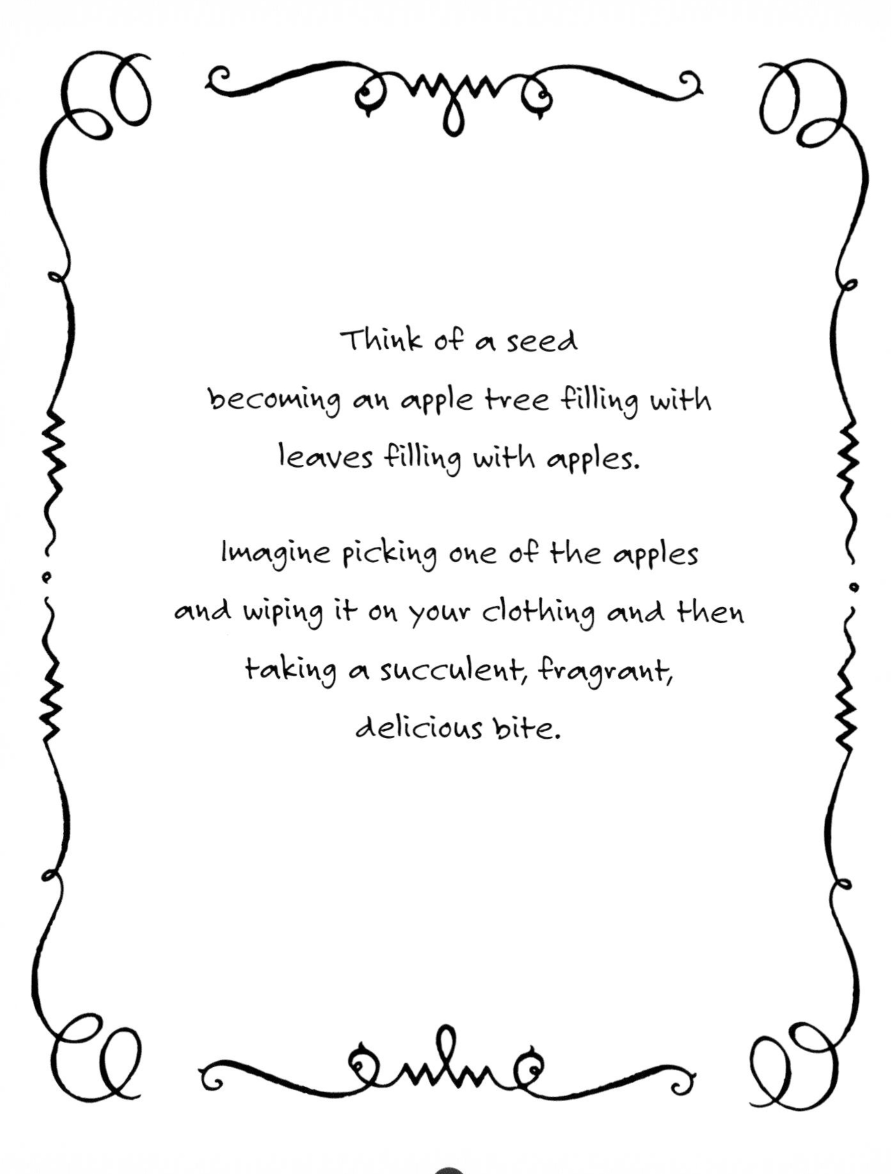

Think of a seed
becoming an apple tree filling with
leaves filling with apples.

Imagine picking one of the apples
and wiping it on your clothing and then
taking a succulent, fragrant,
delicious bite.

Consider the wonder of a rainbow after a storm.

it's there...

Something happens to our senses.
Something happens in our eyes and
our ears, our nose and our mouth,
our skin and . . .
Yes!
In our hearts!

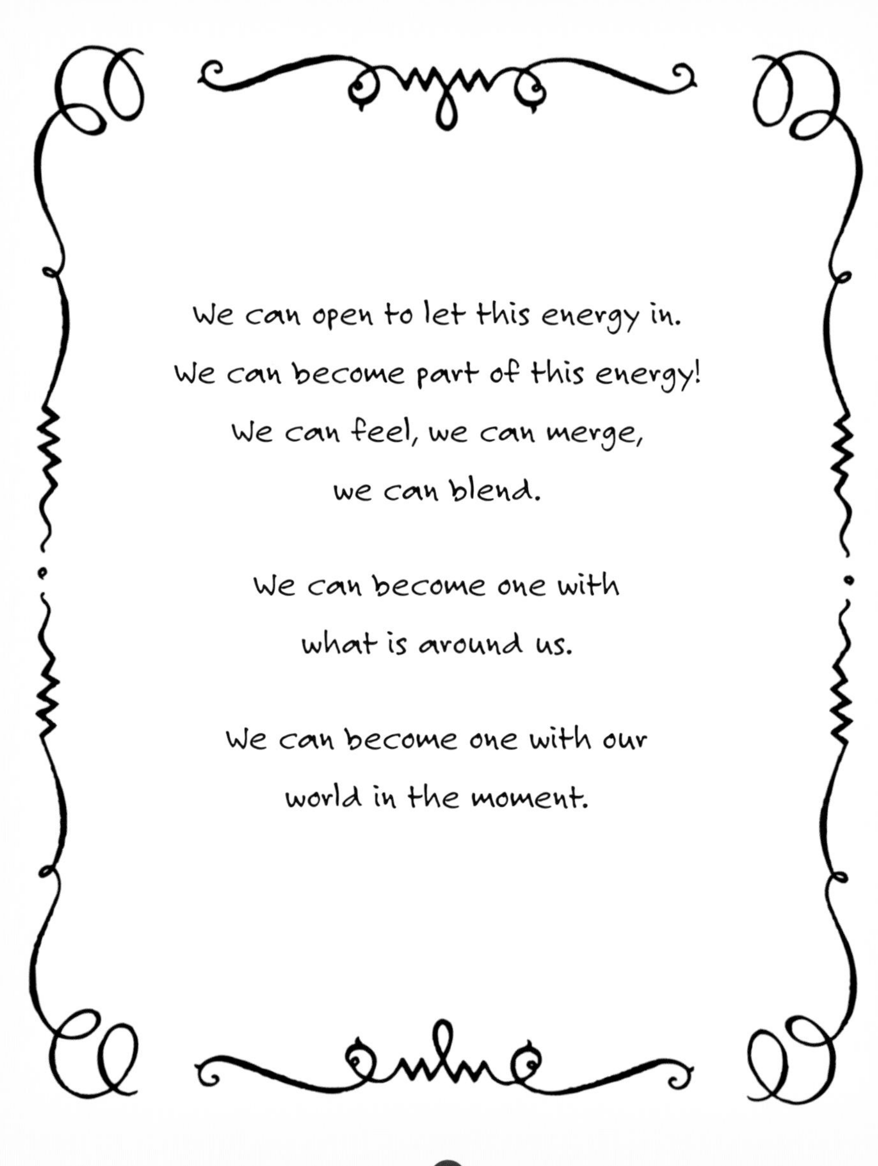

We can open to let this energy in.

We can become part of this energy!

We can feel, we can merge,

we can blend.

We can become one with

what is around us.

We can become one with our

world in the moment.

When we take this time, we discover
in this moment we have nothing to fear,
nothing to worry about, nothing
from which to escape.

In this moment, all that is happening on the planet, in this universe, with our earth is happening as it should happen, and there is nothing we have to do but show up.

be there!

No reason to run away into an
altered state of consciousness,
to hide from this moment.

No reason to

reach for anything else,

want anything else,

need anything else . . .

but this moment.

All we have to do is . . .
Be present.
Breathe.
Be awake.
Be ourselves.
Be here.

here i am.

Be with this page.

Be with your breath.

Be with all of who you are.

Be here

NOW!

Discover what it means to
have a full heart!

it feels good!

An overflowing heart.
A soft heart.
An open heart.

A loving heart.

A joyful heart.

A grateful heart.

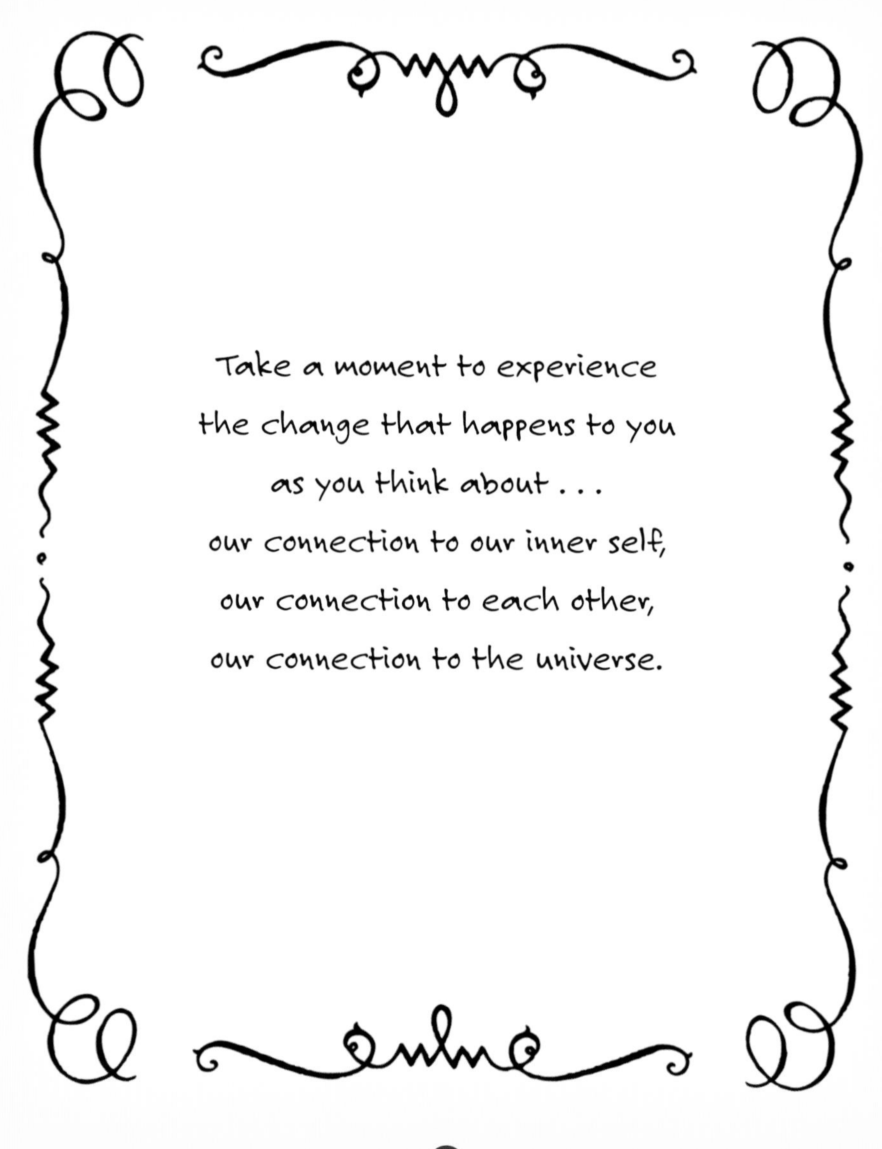

Take a moment to experience
the change that happens to you
as you think about . . .
our connection to our inner self,
our connection to each other,
our connection to the universe.

uniquely beautiful...

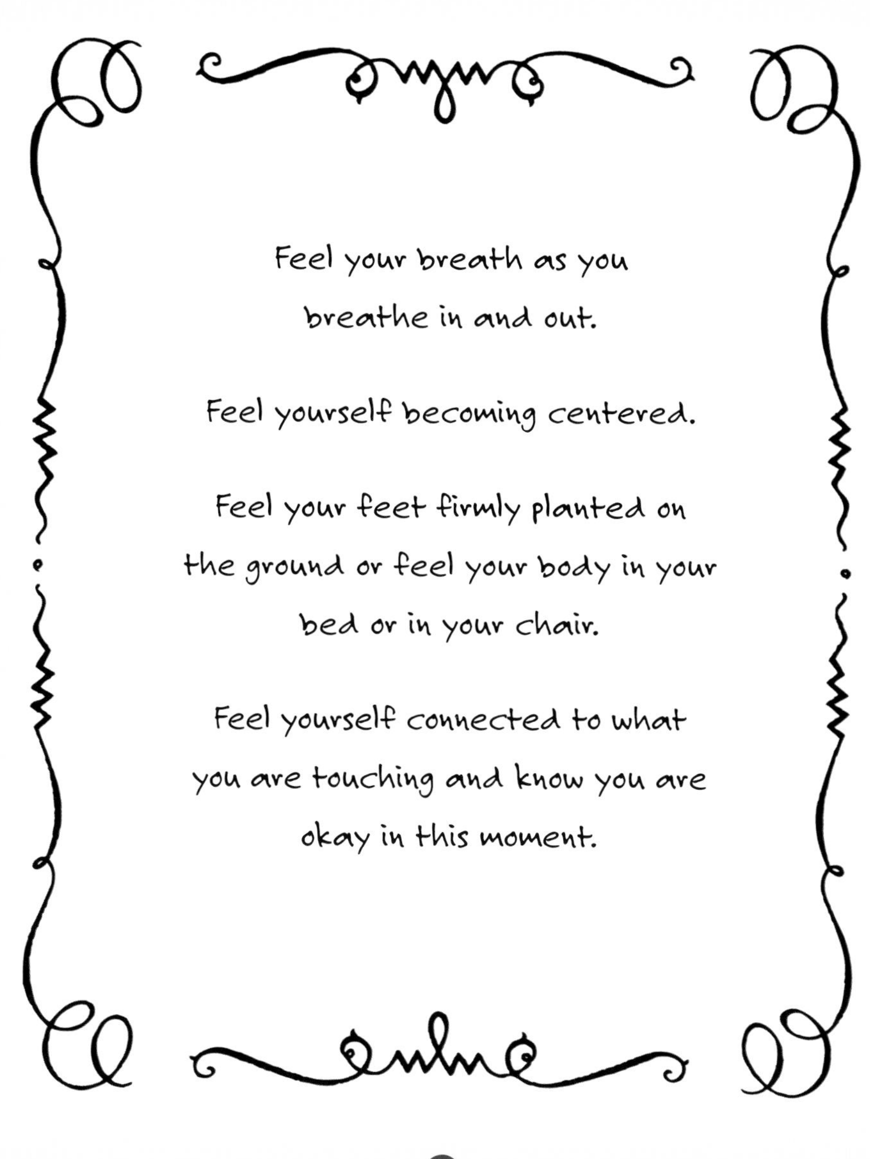

Feel your breath as you
breathe in and out.

Feel yourself becoming centered.

Feel your feet firmly planted on
the ground or feel your body in your
bed or in your chair.

Feel yourself connected to what
you are touching and know you are
okay in this moment.

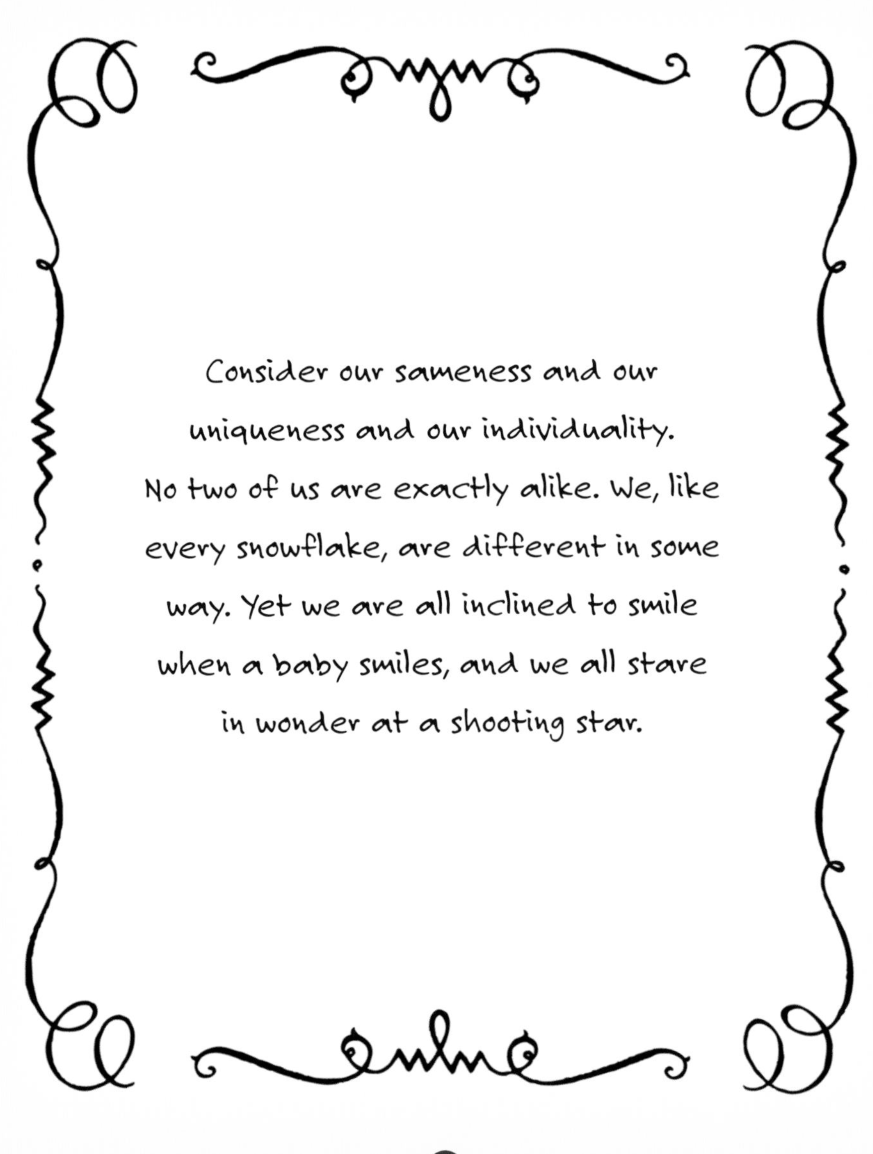

Consider our sameness and our uniqueness and our individuality. No two of us are exactly alike. We, like every snowflake, are different in some way. Yet we are all inclined to smile when a baby smiles, and we all stare in wonder at a shooting star.

Consider why, when it is OUR country winning the Olympics or being the first to land on the moon, we are filled with so much pride.

wow!

Consider why most of us feel warm and alive with the sight of the first spring flower breaking through the cold, hard winter earth.

We are the same and we are different and we all belong to each other and to this universe.

We are all connected to and

by some great power.

Some call it God

or nature . . .

or Allah

or spirituality

or . . .

LOVE.

Yes, some call this power

LOVE.

Some days we explore and wonder.

Some days we take for granted.

There are even days when we

just don't care.

Some of us have been raped or abused and starved
or beaten and neglected or abandoned.

Some us have had fewer opportunities than others.

Some of us have had none.

Some of us have been the victim.
Some the victimizer.

And some of us know that when
any of this is true for any of us,
then we all suffer.

For some of us there are times when
it is so bad, we don't even want to
be here anymore.

And some try to leave.

And some do.

We can be filled with
pain and terror and fear
and agony and sickness
and disease.

We can feel as if we are
on top of the world or in the deepest
darkest hole in the universe.

Our hearts can expand with love
or be closed with misery
or heartache.

But somewhere deep within each
and every one of us, whether we are
rich or poor, sick or healthy, white
or black or red or brown . . .

There is a spark of life and hope

and love, deep, deep inside.

ALIVE!

Waiting, buried deep,

deep, inside.

And if we just stop whenever . . .
however things are . . . but especially
when they are bad . . .

If we just stop and feel our breath and
touch a friend or read this book or hold
a baby or find that rainbow . . .

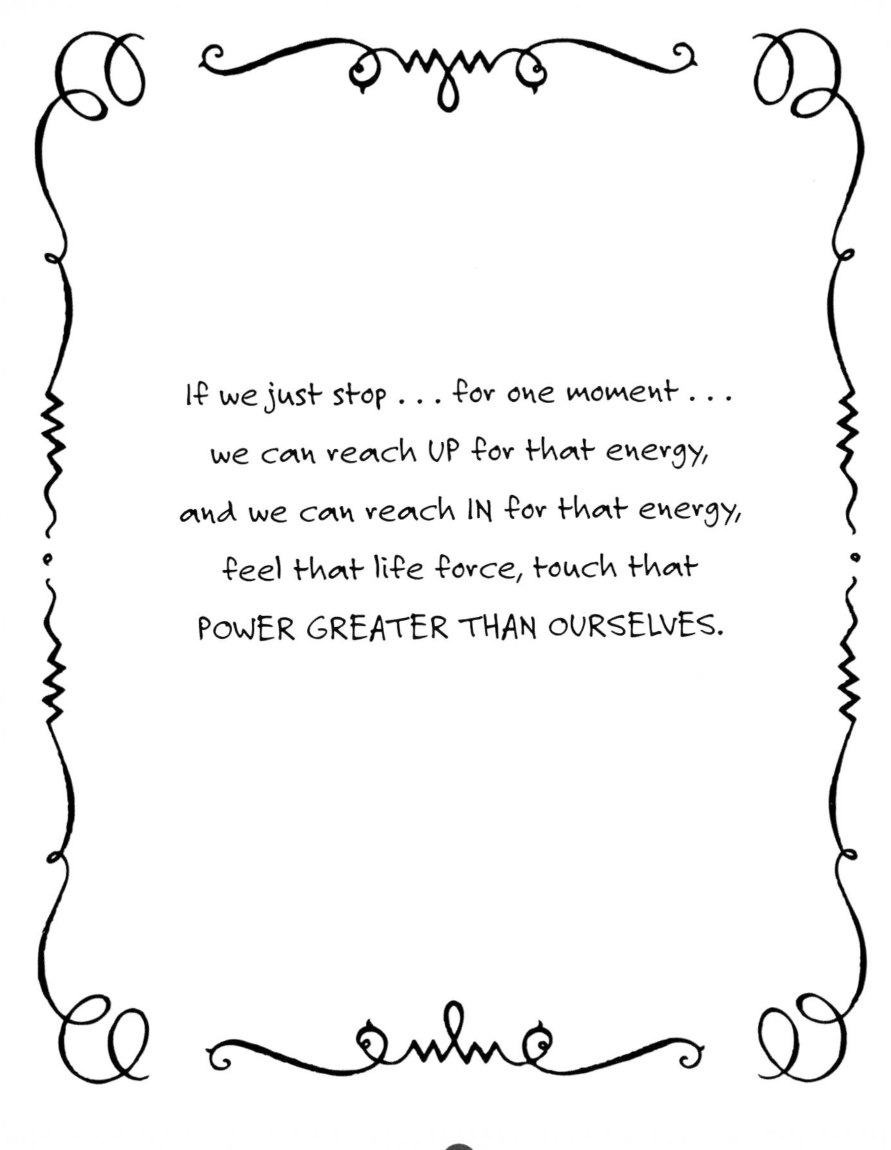

If we just stop . . . for one moment . . .
we can reach UP for that energy,
and we can reach IN for that energy,
feel that life force, touch that
POWER GREATER THAN OURSELVES.

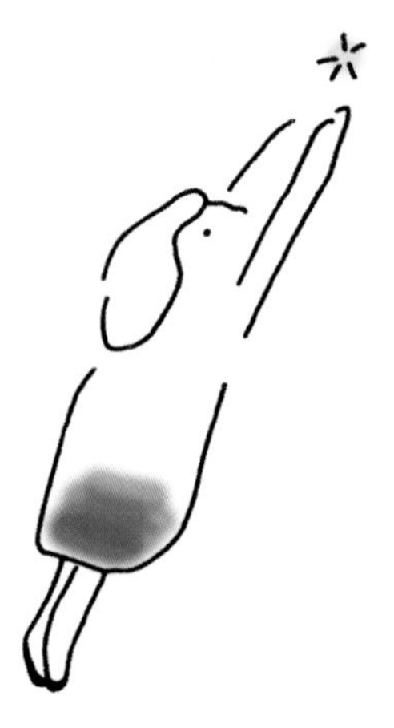

We can reach up and in and
hold on and hang in there.

If we just stop . . .

We can climb up from that dark hole.

And be here. Be present. Be awake

for the next miracle.

Which is

knowing that

WE ARE

the next

MIRACLE.